Learning Short-take®

THE EFFECTIVE LEADER

Skills and tools for inspired leadership

CATHERINE MATTISKE

TPC - The Performance Company Pty Ltd
Level 20, Darling Park
Tower 2, 201 Sussex Street,
Sydney NSW 2000
Australia

ACN 077 455 273
email: tpc@tpc.net.au
Website: www.catherinemattiske.com

© TPC – The Performance Company Pty Limited
First edition published in 2006
Second edition published in 2011
Third edition published in 2022

All rights reserved. Apart from any fair dealing for the purposes of study, research or review, as permitted under Australian copyright law, no part of this publication may be reproduced by any means without the written permission of the copyright owner. Every effort has been made to obtain permission relating to information reproduced in this publication.

The information in this publication is based on the current state of commercial and industry practice, applicable legislation, general law and the general circumstances as at the date of publication. No person shall rely on any of the contents of this publication and the publisher and the author expressly exclude all liability for direct and indirect loss suffered by any person resulting in any way from the use of or reliance on this publication or any part of it. Any options and advice are offered solely in pursuance of the author's and the publisher's intention to provide information, and have not been specifically sought.

For eBook version: By payment of the required fees, you have been granted the non-exclusive, non-transferable right to access and read the text of this e-book on screen. No part of this text may be reproduced, transmitted, downloaded, decompiled, reverse engineered, or stored in or introduced into any information storage retrieval system, in any form or by any means, whether the electronic or mechanical, now known or hereinafter invented, without the express permission of the author.

A catalogue record for this book is available from the National Library of Australia

National Library of Australia
Cataloguing-in-Publication data

Mattiske, Catherine
The Effective Leader: Skills and Tools for Inspired Leadership

ISBN 978-1-921547-18-8

1. Occupational training 2. Learning I. Title

370.113

Distributed by TPC - The Performance Company - www.catherinemattiske.com
For further information contact TPC - The Performance Company, Sydney Australia on +61 (02) 9555 1953.

HELLO.

Welcome to the Learning Short-take® process!

This Learning Short-take® is a bite sized learning package that aims to improve your skills and provide you with an opportunity for personal and professional development to achieve success in your role.

This Learning Short-take® combines self study with workplace activities in a unique learning system to keep you motivated and energized. So let's get started!

Step 1:
What's inside?

- Learning Short-take®. This section contains all of the learning content and will guide you through the learning process.
- Learning Activities. You will be prompted to complete these as you read through.
- Learning Journal. This is a summary of your key learnings. Update it when prompted.
- Skill Development Action Plan. Learning is about taking action. This is your action plan where you'll plan how you will implement your learning.

Step 2:
Complete the Learning Short-take®

- Learning Short-takes® are best completed in a quiet environment that is free of distractions.
- Schedule time in your calendar to complete the Learning Short-take® and prioritize this time as an investment in your own professional development.
- Depending on the title, most participants complete the Learning Short-take® from 90 minutes to 2.5 hours.

Step 3:
Meet with your Manager/Coach

- Schedule a 30 minute meeting with your Manager or Coach.
- At this meeting share your completed Activities, Learning Journal and Skill Development Action Plan.
- Most importantly, discuss and agree on how you will implement your learning in your role.

GET VIP ACCESS
TO YOUR MATERIALS

This Learning Short-take® includes an interactive activity book, associated tools and job aids, plus a bonus eBook.

1 Visit
https://www.catherinemattiske.com/books

2 Select your book

3 Click: **VIP ACCESS**

4 Enter the code: **TEL2022385**

WELCOME

The Effective Leader
Skills and Tools for Inspired Leadership

The Effective Leader will guide managers and leaders at all levels towards maximizing your effectiveness as a leader in the workplace. By demystifying the key concepts of communication, team building, leadership styles, individual and team motivation, performance, and interpersonal skills, you will be better equipped for success in your leadership role.

The Effective Leader covers both the essential theory and practical skills for successful leadership of teams. Through a series of self-assessment and action learning activities you will identify the differences between management and leadership, write vision and mission statements, and identify your natural leadership style. **The Effective Leader** will illustrate how to use additional leadership styles and how to plan and lead effective team meetings.

Increased leadership skills moves individuals and teams to increased resilience in the face of change, enhanced performance and greater success!

The Effective Leader includes the **Meeting Planner, Meeting Agenda, Core Essentials of Compelling Vision & Mission Statements Job Aid**, and the **Leadership Styles Summary**, provided as free downloadable tools.

1	Learning Short-take® Start here
2	Learning Journal 85
3	Skill Development Action Plan 91
4	Quick Reference 97
5	Next Steps 115

> *"The leaders task is to create an environment that is conducive to self motivation."*
>
> — NIDO QUBEIN

Now let's get started!

> *"A leader takes people where they want to go. A great leader takes people where they don't necessarily want to go, but ought to be."*
>
> ROSALYNN CARTER

Section 1

LEARNING SHORT-TAKE®

WHAT'S IN THIS LEARNING SHORT-TAKE®

"Leaders must be close enough to relate to others, but far enough ahead to motivate them."

JOHN MAXWELL

Table of Contents

How to Complete Your Learning Short-take®	5
Activity Checklist	6
Learning Objectives	7
Let's Get Started	8
Part 1 - Getting Started	11
The Effective Leader	12
Part 2 - Management vs Leadership	17
Part 3 - Leadership Vision & Mission	23
Leadership & Vision	24
Leadership & Mission	26
Part 4 - Leadership Styles	31
Leadership Style	32
Using Different Styles	34
How Leadership Styles may be Seen by Others	36
Part 5 - Understanding Behavior	43
Part 6 - Leadership & Roles	49
Leadership & The Theory of Roles	50
Part 7 - Leading a Team	57
Managing Team Meetings	62
Personal and Group Motivation	70

HOW TO COMPLETE YOUR LEARNING SHORT-TAKE®

1. **Reflect on your skills and abilities** in leadership and how you use this information to improve effectiveness in your role.

2. **Complete the Leadership Self & Organizational Assessment.**

3. Highlight specific skill areas that you believe you could develop more. Add these to your **Learning Journal** as you go.

4. When you have completed this Learning Short-take® **meet with your Manager/Coach.** In this meeting, you will jointly establish a personal **Skill Development Action Plan.**

5. **Subject to your coach's final review** and assessment, you will either sign off the module, or undertake further skill development as appropriate.

"Vision without action is merely a dream. Action without vision just passes the time. Vision with action can change the world."

JOEL BARKER - POWER OF VISION

ACTIVITY CHECKLIST

"A business is a reflection of the leader."

GARY FELDMAR

During this Learning Short-take® you will be prompted to complete the following activities:

- Activity 1 -   Leadership Self & Organizational Assessment   9
- Activity 2 -   Your Leadership Role   21
- Activity 3 -   Vision & Mission   28
- Activity 4 -   Style Analysis   38
- Activity 5 -   Leadership Style Reflections   41
- Activity 6 -   Team Behavior - Leadership Language   48
- Activity 7 -   Team Roles   55
- Activity 8 -   Meeting Planner   68
- Activity 9 -   Meeting Agenda   69
- Activity 10 - Your Motivators   79
- Activity 11 - Analyzing Team Motivation   82
- Activity 12 - Motivating Ways   83
- Activity 13 - Inspiring Through Vision   84
- Learning Journal   85
- Skill Development Action Plan   91

LEARNING OBJECTIVES

After you have completed this Learning Short-take®, you should be able to:

- Define the relationship between leadership and management.
- Understand the meaning of vision, mission and values.
- Know the role of leader as coach.
- Apply the theory of the functional and situational approaches to leadership.
- Work on the personal qualities of leadership and display the will to lead.
- Have a high regard for communication in the leadership process and develop the ability to communicate.
- List ways to influence motivation for each member of your team.
- Create a Skill Development Action Plan

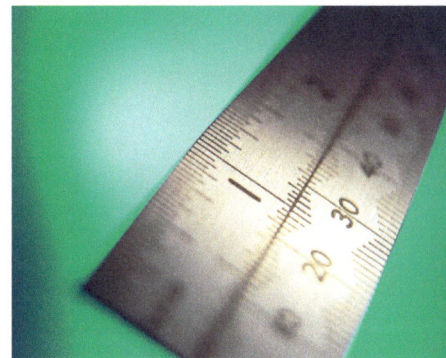

"Managers are people who do things right, while leaders are people who do the right thing."

WARREN BENNIS, PH.D.
"ON BECOMING A LEADER"

LET'S GET STARTED

The successful organization has one major attribute that sets it apart from unsuccessful organizations: dynamic and effective leadership.

Peter F Drucker (a leading author on leadership) pointed out that managers (business leaders) are a basic and scarce resource of any business enterprise.

Businesses are continually searching for effective leaders, and they are not easy to find. This shortage of effective leadership is not confined to business but is evident in every other form of organization.

Building leadership skills and knowledge is essential for business growth and the achievement of personal and organizational goals.

"Leadership and learning are indispensable to each other."
JOHN F. KENNEDY

Complete Activity # 1
Leadership Self & Organizational Assessment

ACTIVITY 1: LEADERSHIP SELF & ORGANIZATIONAL ASSESSMENT

A leader is a person that inspires you to take a journey to a destination you would not go to by yourself. Traditional managers who maintain the status quo and fail to inspire their people will not be effective in today's environment. Effective leadership is about change, innovation, passion and creativity.

As times change, leadership skills must also change. What was successful in the past may still relevant, but may not be everything needed for the future. Use this assessment to rate your organization and yourself. You can also give it to others and have them provide you an honest appraisal.

Scoring Directions: Rate yourself AND your organization on a score of 1 (lowest) - 5 (highest) for each item.

	Description	Score Your Organization	Score Yourself
Process Management	Designs and manages processes that are efficient and effective. These processes support the delivery of either the organization's service or the manufacture of the organization's products. Processes move horizontally across organizational boundaries. Score yourself higher if you have identified your critical processes.		
Customer Driven	One of the highest leadership priorities is the ability to focus on the needs and expectations of customers. Do you build and maintain relationships with customers? Do you have systems in place to measure customer satisfaction and customer loyalty? (Customers can also be employees) Add points if you know the needs, expectations and desires of your customers. Deduct points if there are only certain select parts of the organization having this information.		
Information Management	The innovative organization thrives on information. There are multiple avenues and many means of expressing the goals, plans, and status of the organization to all people working within it. The organization shares success stories and ideas with everyone. How many means are available to improve communication? For example, meetings, online / digital / project management software, bulletin boards, email etc. Score yourself lower if there is no organized system in place to spread information.		
Change Management	A leader of the organization is knowledgeable of, and manages change appropriately, dovetailing management philosophies into the strategic or business planning. Deduct more points if your last change action created anger, resentment and frustration.		

ACTIVITY 1: CONTINUED

	Description	Score Your Organization	Score Yourself
Innovation	Makes focused efforts to initiate new ideas and suggestions. The leader is constantly looking at other industries and trends to see beyond the horizon for new ways to do things. The organization does not maintain status quo. Add one point if people from your organization have taken site visits or bench marked other organizations during the past six months.		
Continuous Improvement	Continuously improving everything the enterprise does. Processes and procedures are constantly being improved. Score yourself higher if you have a continuous improvement program. Deduct one point if it is only a "suggestion box."		
Obstacle Removal	The innovative leader spends time pinpointing and removing barriers and obstacles obstructing work flow. Employees feel free to go to anyone in the organization for advice and assistance. Deduct points if you have not had an employee survey or sensing session during the past year.		
Charts the Course	Provides a clear direction toward the future. Are you enthusiastic and inspiring others to take a journey to a particular destination? If there is no clear direction or inspiring vision, mark yourself low. Give yourself points if people are involved in the goal setting process.		
Provides Motivation	You have a system of reward and recognition. Team based rewards lead to higher morale. Employees feel that they are contributing to the vitality of the enterprise. Give yourself two points if you have provided recognition to a worker or team during the past five days. Reduce points if you only recognise length of service.		
Trust Builder	This leader allows people to learn from their mistakes and allows risk taking. The leader who tolerates risk taking scores higher in innovation. Bad signs – more than two signatures on any form, too many auditors and inspectors and time clocks.		
Provides Purpose	Purpose gives people a reason why they should work for this organization. People relate best to the organization when they understand how their actions relate to the big picture. The person who understands how their actions affect the organization is more empowered to take action.		
	TOTAL SCORE		

SCORING:
75+ = Admirable Leadership Skills: Enhance & Hone Opportunities
51-74 = Skillful Leadership: Growth Opportunities
35-50 = Average Leadership Skills: Improvement Opportunities
<35 = Inexpert Skills: Significant Improvement Opportunities

Personal development plan ideas:
1 _____
2 _____

Now update your Learning Journal (page 85)

GETTING STARTED

PART 1

THE EFFECTIVE LEADER

Leadership Defined

Leadership is the process of directing the behavior of others toward the accomplishment of some common objectives. Leadership is influencing people to get things done willingly, and to a standard and quality above their norm.

As an element in social interaction, leadership is a complex activity involving influence, striving for the achievement of goals, team commitment and the reinforcement or changing of organizational culture.

Managers have subordinates

By definition, managers have subordinates - unless their title is honorary and given as a mark of seniority.

Authoritarian, transactional style

Managers have a position of authority vested in them by the company. Those that work for them largely do as they are told. Management style is transactional, in that the manager tells the subordinate what to do.

Work focus

Managers are paid to get things done (they are subordinates too), often within tight constraints of time and money. In turn they pass on this work focus to their subordinates.

Leaders have followers

When leaders are leading they do not have subordinates they have followers. Many organizational leaders do have subordinates, but only because they are also managers. When leaders want to lead, they have to give up formal authoritarian control, because to lead is to have followers, and following is always a voluntary activity.

Transformational style
Telling people what to do does not inspire them to follow you. You have to appeal to them, showing how following them will lead to their hearts' desire. They must want to follow you enough to stop what they are doing and perhaps confront situations that they would not normally consider risking.

People focus
Although many leaders have a charismatic style to some extent, this does not require a loud personality. They are always good with people. Leaders give credit to others, accept responsibility, and are very effective at creating loyalty.

Although leaders are good with people, limits need to be set on how friendly they are with their followers. In order to keep the mystique of leadership, they often retain a degree of separation and aloofness.

This does not mean that leaders do not pay attention to tasks - in fact they are often very achievement-focused. What they do realize, however, is the importance of enthusing others to work towards their vision.

Seek risk
When pursuing their vision, leaders consider it natural to encounter problems and hurdles that must be overcome along the way. Leaders seem more comfortable with risk, seeking opportunities and alternate ways of doing things that others may avoid.

Effective Leadership as a Source of Competitive Business Advantage

Leadership is imperative for moulding a group of people into a team and shaping them into a force that creates competitive business advantage.

Leaders know how to make people function in a collaborative fashion, and how to motivate them to excel their performance. Leaders also know how to balance the individual team member's ambition with the goal of producing synergy - an outcome that exceeds the sum of individual parts.

- The role of a leader is to create followers.
- The task of a leader is to bring about constructive and necessary change.
- The responsibility of a leader is to bring about the change in a way that is responsive to the objectives and long-term needs of all stakeholders.

Learning to Lead

Effective leaders recognise that what they know is very little in comparison to what they still need to learn. To be more proficient in pursuing and achieving objectives, you should be open to new ideas, insights, and revelations that can lead to better ways to accomplishing goals. Continuous improvement can be put into practice through engaging yourself in a constant dialogue with your peers, advisers, consultants, team members, suppliers, customers, and competitors. Leading others is not simply a matter of style, or following how-to guides or recipes. The ineffectiveness of leaders seldom results from a lack of know-how or how-to, nor is it typically due to inadequate managerial skills.

Leadership is more than creating a great vision. Leadership is also about creating conditions under which all your followers can perform independently and effectively toward a common objective.

Effective leaders establish values, model behaviors, encourage and reward followers, and in many ways foster

self-leadership in individuals and teams that develop the organizational culture. An important measure of a leader's own success is the success of his or her followers. The strength of a leader is measured by the ability to facilitate others. If leaders want to lead somebody, they must first lead themselves.

Attributes & Competencies Balanced with Results

Leadership attributes are the inner or personal qualities that constitute effective leadership. These attributes include a large array of characteristics such as personal values, character, motives, habits, traits, style, behaviors and skills.

Leadership competencies such as vision, character, trust, and other exemplary attributes, competencies and capabilities underpin the day-to-day effectiveness of leaders.

Organizational capabilities together with the leader's attributes and competencies are directly linked to desired results. By improving your leadership abilities you will maximise the chances of enhancing the performance of your team and in turn meet your personal and organizational goals.

Now update your Learning Journal (page 85)

"

"All of the great leaders have had one characteristic in common; it was the willingness to confront unequivocally the major anxiety of their people in their time. This, and not much else, is the essence of leadership."

JOHN KENNETH GALBRAITH

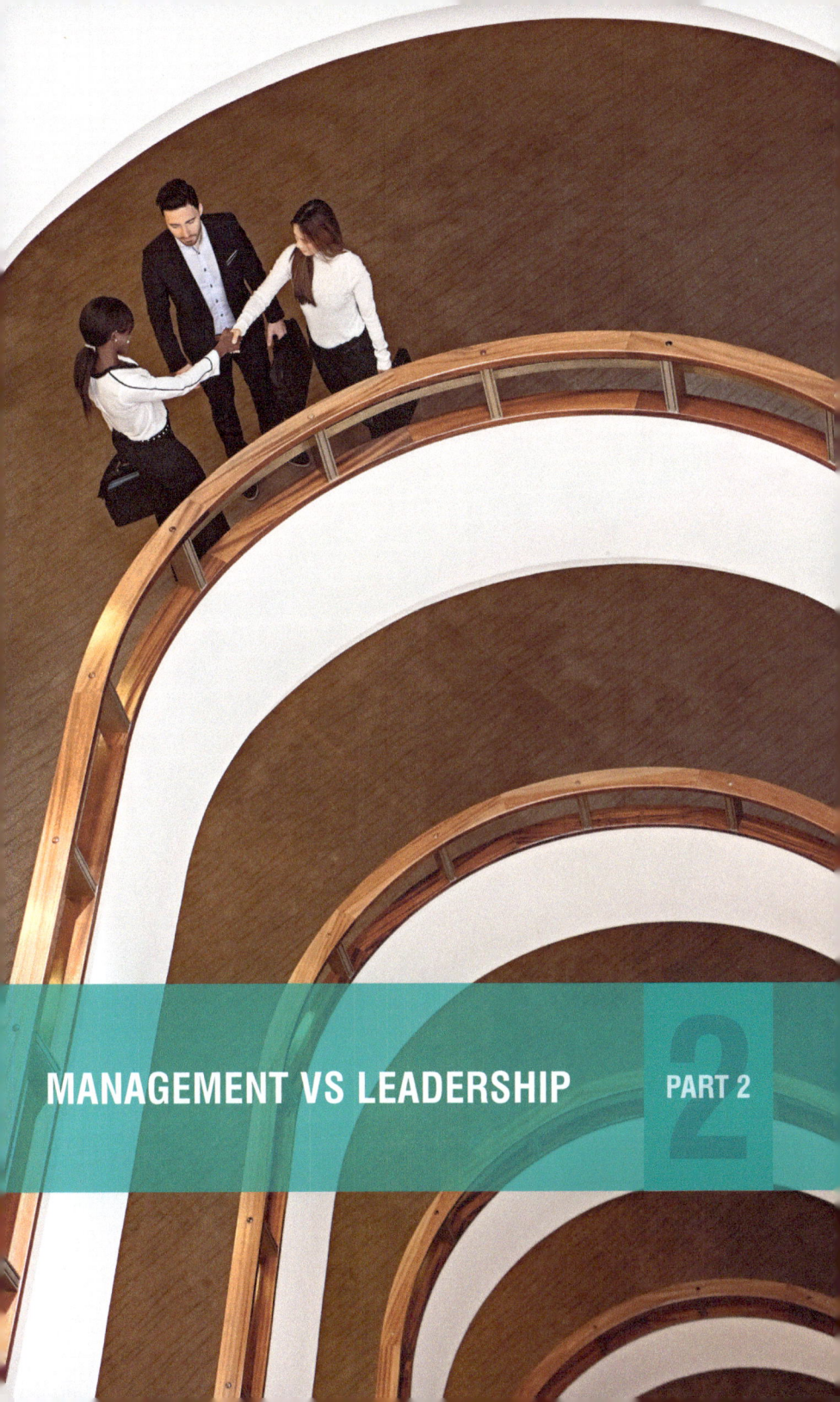

MANAGEMENT VS LEADERSHIP

PART 2

MANAGEMENT VS LEADERSHIP

Management =
day-to-day operational tasks

Leadership =
influencing for long-term goal achievement

"Management is efficiency in climbing the ladder of success; leadership determines whether the ladder is leaning against the right wall."

STEPHEN R. COVEY

Management and leadership are often thought of as one and the same thing, however there is an important distinction between the two. In essence, leadership is a broader concept than management.

Management is the managing of day-to-day operational tasks, for example, managing projects, finance, staff, administration and so on.

Leadership occurs whenever one person attempts to influence the behavior of an individual or group, regardless of the reason. It may be for one's own goals or for the goals of others and these goals should be congruent with organizational goals.

Leadership - 4 Definitions

The Collins English Dictionary.
(© 2022 HarperCollins Publishers)

Leadership (n)
1. The position or function of a leader.
2. The period during which a person occupies the position of leader.
3. a. the ability to lead. b. (as modifier): leadership qualities.
4. the leaders as a group of a party, union, etc.

This dictionary definition of leadership focuses on the position (singular or collective), tenure and ability of leaders. As such, it misses key points about the purpose and hallmarks of effective leadership.

Peter F Drucker suggests:

"The only definition of a leader is someone who has followers."

To gain followers requires influence (see John Maxwell's definition below) but doesn't exclude the lack of integrity in achieving this. Indeed, it can be argued that several of the world's greatest leaders have lacked integrity and have adopted values that would not be shared by many people today.

John C Maxwell advocates:

"Leadership is influence - nothing more, nothing less."

This moves beyond the position defining the leader, to looking at the ability of the leader to influence others - both those who would consider themselves followers, and those outside that circle. Indirectly, it also builds in leadership character, since without maintaining integrity and trustworthiness, the capability to influence will disappear.

Warren Bennis proposes:

"Leadership is a function of knowing yourself, having a vision that is well communicated, building trust among colleagues, and taking effective action to realize your own leadership potential."

"The task of the leader is to get his people from where they are to where they have not been."

HENRY KISSINGER

Complete Activity # 2
Your Leadership Role

ACTIVITY 2: YOUR LEADERSHIP ROLE

(a) - Define Leadership

Using the four definitions provided, create your own definition of leadership.

_____

_____

_____

_____

_____

(b) - Your Management vs Your Leadership Role

In the table below, list your current management responsibilities and your leadership initiatives over the last 12 months. (If you are new to your organization, consider previous leadership roles)

Management Responsibilities	Leadership Initiatives – The Past 12 months

Now update your Learning Journal (page 85)

"

"To lead people, walk beside them ...
As for the best leaders,
the people do not notice their existence.
The next best, the people honor and praise.
The next, the people fear;
and the next, the people hate ...
When the best leader's work is done the people say,
'We did it ourselves!'"

LAO-TSU

LEADERSHIP VISION & MISSION
PART 3

LEADERSHIP & VISION

All organizations start with someone having an idea. The leaders within the organization need to share this idea or vision. To turn this vision into results, leaders need assistance from others.

In order to achieve this, the vision needs to be articulated so that others can see the possibility of realizing the potential.

What is Vision?

Vision is more about motivating people than about providing them with direction. The emotionally expressed intention to be the best XYZ in the world is inspiring. It gives people something to believe in, to work towards, and to identify with. **The Vision is the goal**.

Without direction - leadership - the vision is just wishful thinking. Vision is not, in itself, leadership. More precisely, HAVING a vision is not leadership. Simply expressing a vision enthusiastically amounts to being a cheerleader - a good motivator.

Vision is a good tool for motivating people. Having the company vision displayed prominently within the working environment and visible within the company continuously reminds people where they are headed and seeks to provide an aim. This acts as motivation for people to strive to meet the vision.

Vision comes from the top. It is the responsibility of top management to create a vision for the organization and to articulate this vision in a relatable way. In doing so, it turns into concrete strategies, solid management systems and informed resource allocations that enable an organization to accomplish results.

Being Active with the Vision

The active component of a leaders role is the accountability and responsibility for modelling behavior. For a vision to be successful, the leadership needs to walk the talk.

It is essential to appreciate that all members of an organization have an integral role to play in realizing the organization's vision. Leaders in particular are responsible for facilitating this vision as it is presented through the mission down through behaviors and task/people management.

The Primary Purpose of a Vision Statement

The primary purpose of a vision statement is to describe the organizations intent with regard to the future it desires to create. It makes a compelling statement about what the company is striving to achieve. It is usually brief, concise and easy to remember.

The vision should primarily address the needs of employees, shareholders and society. They all want to know if the future of the company resonates with their motivation and needs. The vision is particularly important for employees, because it describes where the company might take them.

Example of a Vision Statement

To be the premier customer-driven real estate service company.

Vision vs. Mission

The vision represents a deeper level of motivation than a mission. The mission describes the 'means', the vision describes the 'end'.

LEADERSHIP & MISSION

"Leadership: The art of getting someone else to do something you want done because he wants to do it."

DWIGHT EISENHOWER

Mission Statement Purpose

Mission statements do two things: 1) They keep the energies of the company focused around its core business, and 2) they motivate stakeholders. The Mission Statement should be concise, inclusive and easily memorized.

The mission statement should be communicated to employees, customers, shareholders and increasingly the broader community. It is a very visible commitment to the achievement of the organization's vision.

Four Objectives of a Mission

1) It clearly states the company's core business

2) It clearly states how the organization's vision will be met

3) It inspires customers

4) It encourages employees.

Mission Statement Example # 1

Our business is renting cars; our mission is total customer satisfaction.

This mission statement identifies the core business, and it leaves customers in no doubt that the company cares about their needs. It sends a strong message to its employees that caring for customers is the company's number one concern.

Mission Statement Example # 2

We will achieve our goal to provide society with superior products and services through innovations and solutions that satisfy customer's needs and improve the quality of life. We will provide employees with meaningful work and advancement opportunities, and investors with a superior rate of return.

"A good leader can't get too far ahead of his followers."

FRANKLIN D. ROOSEVELT

Complete Activity # 3
Vision & Mission

To help you with this activity, download the job aid: **CORE Essentials of Compelling Vision & Mission Statements** from https://www.catherinematttiske.com/books

© 2022, TPC - The Performance Company Pty Limited. All rights reserved.

ACTIVITY 3: VISION AND MISSION

(a) - Vision and Mission Research

Most organizations publish their vision and mission on their web sites. Search the internet for six companies and find their vision and mission statements. Perhaps begin with your competitors, similar size organizations to yours, fast-growing organizations, blue-chip corporations or others categories that suit your purpose.

Write their Vision and Mission in the table below.

Company Name	Vision	Mission	Comments (like/dislikes)
1.			
2.			
3.			
4.			
5.			
6.			

ACTIVITY 3: CONTINUED

(b) - Your Vision and Mission

Regardless of your leadership role within your organization you can create a vision and mission statement. If you are the business owner, managing director or other senior leader write a vision and mission statement for the entire organization. If you lead a team, department or a part of the organization write the vision and mission statement for that part of the organization which you lead.

In preparation for writing your vision focus on your business (or your team).

Remember your vision (your goal) and mission (how you will achieve your goal) needs to motivate and meet the needs of the organization, team, society.

You may choose to put a time frame around the vision (e.g. "Within 3 years we will…"), or create a more timeless vision statement.

1 - Write Your Vision

2 - Write Your Mission

3 - Vision and Mission Communication Strategy

Who should know about the vision and mission? How will you communicate your vision and mission?

Stakeholder Group	Communication Method

Now update your Learning Journal (page 85)

"
"An empowered organization is one in which individuals have the knowledge, skill, desire, and opportunity to personally succeed in a way that leads to collective organizational success."

STEPHEN R. COVEY, PRINCIPLE-CENTERED LEADERSHIP

"

LEADERSHIP STYLES

PART 4

LEADERSHIP STYLE

Leadership style is the manner and approach of providing direction, implementing plans, and motivating people. The model shows three different styles of leadership: authoritarian (autocratic), participative (democratic), and delegative (free reign).

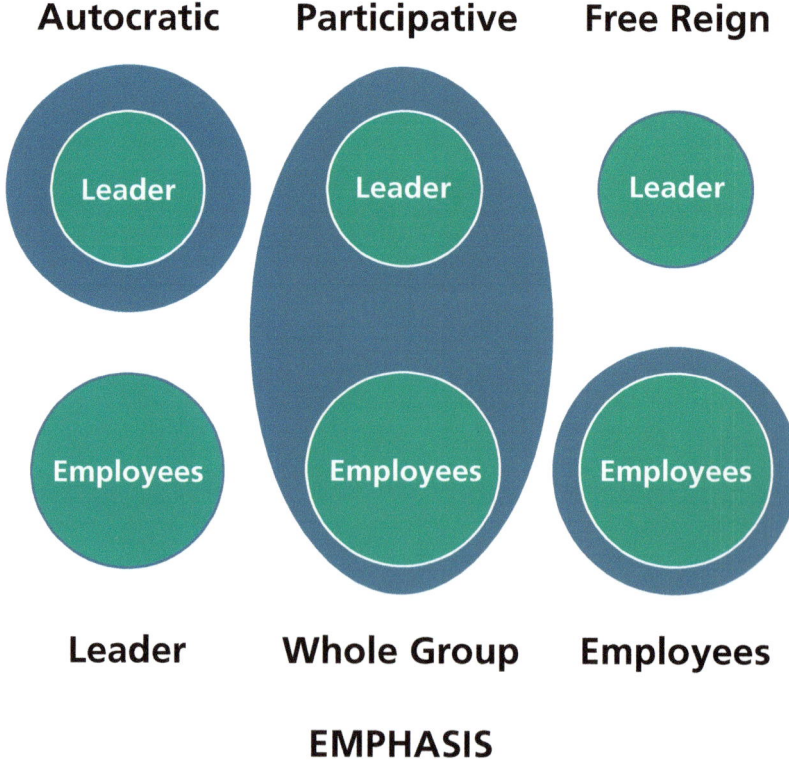

EMPHASIS

Although most leaders use all three styles, one of them usually becomes the dominate one.

Authoritarian (Autocratic)

This type is used when the leader tells employees what to do and how it is to be done, without getting the advice of the individual or team. Some of the appropriate conditions to use it is when you have all the information to solve the problem, you are short on time, and your employees are well motivated.

Some people think that this style includes yelling, using demeaning language, and leading by threats and abuse of power. This is not the authoritarian style… it is an abusive, unprofessional style of leadership.

Participative (Democratic)

Participative leadership style involves the leader including one or more employees in on the decision making process (determining what to do and how to do it). However, the leader maintains the final decision and maintains authority.

The participative leadership style may be used when you have some of the information, and your employees have some of the information. This allows them to become part of the decision making process and allows you to make a better decision.

Delegative (Free Reign)

In this style, the leader allows the employees to make the decision. However, the leader is still responsible for the decisions made. This is used when employees are able to analyze the situation and determine what needs to be done and how to do it. As a leader it is important to remember that you can't do everything! You must set priorities and delegate certain tasks.

USING DIFFERENT STYLES

A good leader uses all three styles, depending on what situations arise.

The Authoritarian Style

The authoritarian style is often used with a new employee who is learning the job. In this situation the leader needs to be competent with the task and a good coach. The new employee is usually motivated to learn a new skill.

For example, in the event that a procedure is not working the authoritarian style would be to tell the team that a procedure is not working correctly and a new one must be established. The leader would have devised the new procedure and tells the team to implement it.

The Participative Style

The participative style is best used with a team of workers who know their job yet still look to the leader for the final decision. The leader needs to know the problem or task well, but wants to create a team where the employees take ownership of the project. The participative style takes more time than authoritarian however builds the foundation for long-term ownership.

For example, in the event that a procedure is not working the participative style would be to meet with the team (or key members of the team) and ask for their ideas and input on creating a new procedure. The leader would then decide the way forward and implement the change of procedure.

The Delegative Style

The delegative style is the ideal choice when an employee knows more about the job than the leader. By having a team of people who take ownership of their job and who share in the responsibility of the business results means that the leader can be working at other places doing other things or taking the time for strategic planning.

For example, in the event that a procedure is not working the delegative style would assign the task of creating and implementing the new procedure and report on its progress.

Choosing Leadership Style

The effective leader should use all three leadership styles and will choose the most appropriate style for each situation. Some of the criteria for choosing the appropriate style include:

- How much time is available?
- Are relationships based on respect and trust or on disrespect?
- Who has the information - you, your employees, or both?
- How well are your employees trained and how well do you know the task?
- Are there internal conflicts that are in place or may result?
- What would be the impact to existing or future stress levels?
- What is the type of task: structured, unstructured, complicated, or simple?
- What are the governing laws or established procedures?

HOW LEADERSHIP STYLES MAY BE SEEN BY OTHERS

Effective leaders use a mix of authoritarian, participative and delegative leadership styles. The key is to match your leadership style with the situation and the skill of your employees. If you match well your leadership style will appear to be effective for the employee.

If you use the wrong style for a particular situation, your employees may see you as being ineffective.

Basic Style	Effective	Ineffective
Authoritarian	Seen as having well-defined methods for accomplishing goals that are helpful to followers.	Seen as imposing methods on others; sometimes seen as unpleasant and interested only in short-run output.
Participative	Seen as satisfying the needs of the group for setting goals and organizing work, but also providing high levels of socio-emotional support.	Seen as initiating more structure than is needed by the group and often appears not to be genuine in interpersonal relationships.
Delegative	Seen as appropriately delegating to followers decisions about how the work should be done and providing little socio-emotional support where little is needed by the group.	Seen as providing little structure or socio-emotional support when needed by members of the group.

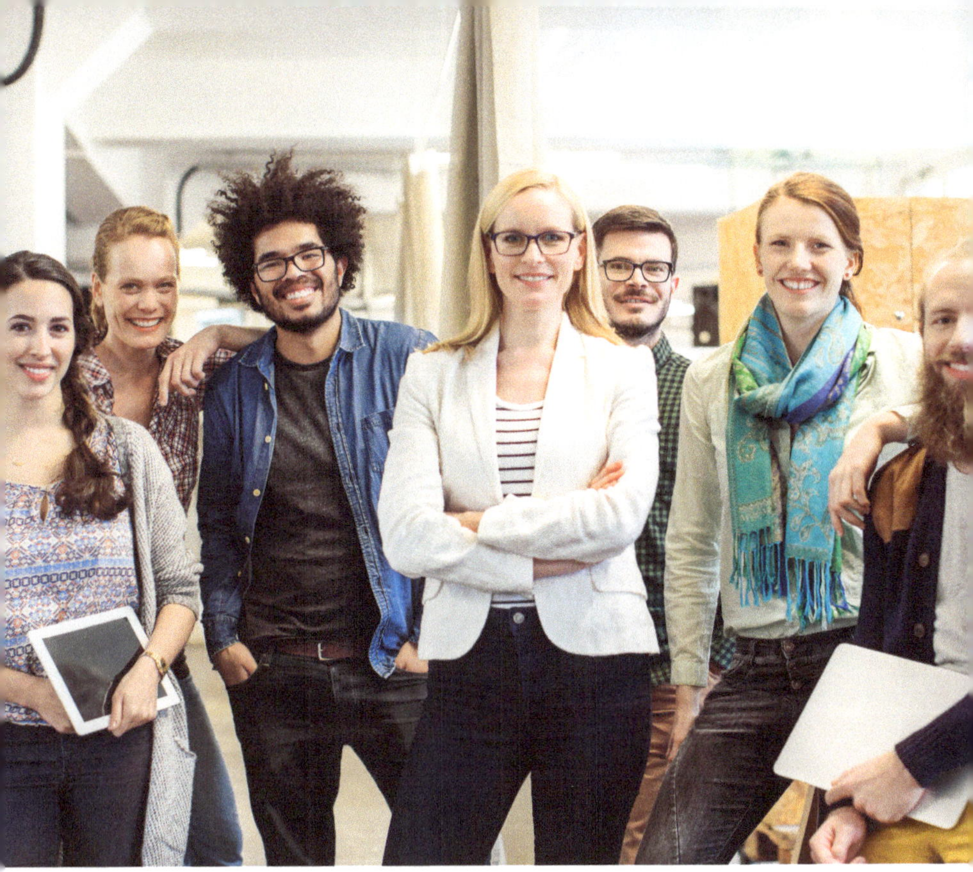

"The greater the loyalty of a group toward the group, the greater is the motivation among the members to achieve the goals of the group, and the greater the probability that the group will achieve its goals."

RENSIS LIKERT

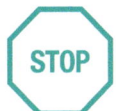

STOP

Complete Activity # 4

Style Analysis

STOP

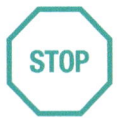

Complete Activity # 5

Leadership Style

ACTIVITY 4: STYLE ANALYSIS

This questionnaire contains statements about leadership style beliefs. Be honest about your choices as there are no right or wrong answers - it is only for your own self-assessment.

Next to each statement, circle the number that represents how strongly you feel about the statement by using the following scoring system:

Almost Always True = 5, Frequently True = 4, Occasionally True = 3, Seldom True = 2, Almost Never True = 1

	Almost Always True	Frequently True	Occasionally True	Seldom True	Almost Never True
1. I always retain the final decision making authority within my department or team.	5	4	3	2	1
2. I always try to include one or more employees in determining what to do and how to do it. However, I maintain the final decision making authority.	5	4	3	2	1
3. I and my employees always vote whenever a major decision has to be made.	5	4	3	2	1
4. I do not consider suggestions made by my employees as I do not have the time for them.	5	4	3	2	1
5. I ask for employee ideas and input on upcoming plans and projects.	5	4	3	2	1
6. For a major decision to pass in my department, it must have the approval of each individual or the majority.	5	4	3	2	1
7. I tell my employees what has to be done and how to do it.	5	4	3	2	1
8. When things go wrong and I need to create a strategy to keep a project or process running on schedule, I call a meeting to get my employee's advice.	5	4	3	2	1
9. To get information out, I send it by email, phone/voicemail, or digitally (E.g. video message); very rarely is a meeting called. My employees are then expected to act upon the information.	5	4	3	2	1
10. When someone makes a mistake, I tell them not to ever do that again and make a note of it.	5	4	3	2	1
11. I want to create an environment where the employees take ownership of the project. I allow them to participate in the decision making process.	5	4	3	2	1
12. I allow my employees to determine what needs to be done and how to do it.	5	4	3	2	1
13. New hires are not allowed to make any decisions unless it is approved by me first.	5	4	3	2	1

ACTIVITY 4: CONTINUED

	Almost Always True	Frequently True	Occasionally True	Seldom True	Almost Never True
14. I ask employees for their vision of where they see their jobs going and then use their vision where appropriate.	5	4	3	2	1
15. My workers know more about their jobs than me, so I allow them to carry out the decision to do their job.	5	4	3	2	1
16. When something goes wrong, I tell my employees that a procedure is not working correctly and I establish a new one.	5	4	3	2	1
17. I allow my employees to set priorities with my guidance.	5	4	3	2	1
18. I delegate tasks in order to implement a new procedure or process.	5	4	3	2	1
19. I closely monitor my employees to ensure they are performing correctly.	5	4	3	2	1
20. When there are differences in role expectations, I work with them to resolve the differences.	5	4	3	2	1
21. Each individual is responsible for defining their job.	5	4	3	2	1
22. I like the power that my leadership position holds over subordinates.	5	4	3	2	1
23. I like to use my leadership power to help subordinates grow.	5	4	3	2	1
24. I like to share my leadership power with my subordinates.	5	4	3	2	1
25. Employees must be directed or threatened with negative consequences in order to get them to achieve the organizational objectives.	5	4	3	2	1
26. Employees will exercise self-direction if they are committed to the objectives.	5	4	3	2	1
27. Employees have the right to determine their own organizational objectives.	5	4	3	2	1
28. Employees seek mainly security.	5	4	3	2	1
29. Employees know how to use creativity and ingenuity to solve organizational problems.	5	4	3	2	1
30. My employees can lead themselves just as well as I can.	5	4	3	2	1

© 2022, TPC - The Performance Company Pty Limited. All rights reserved.

ACTIVITY 4: SCORING

Score of each item on the questionnaire. For example, if you scored item 1 with a 3 (Occasionally), write 3 next to Item 1. When you have entered all the scores for each question, total each of the three columns.

Item	Score	Item	Score	Item	Score
1	____	2	____	3	____
4	____	5	____	6	____
7	____	8	____	9	____
10	____	11	____	12	____
13	____	14	____	15	____
16	____	17	____	18	____
19	____	20	____	21	____
22	____	23	____	24	____
25	____	26	____	27	____
28	____	29	____	30	____
TOTAL	____	TOTAL	____	TOTAL	____
Authoritarian Style (autocratic)		Participative Style (democratic)		Delegative Style (free reign)	

This questionnaire is to help you assess what leadership style you normally use. The lowest score possible for a stage is 10 (Almost never) while the highest score possible for a stage is 50 (Almost always).

Identify Your Leadership Style

- The **highest** of the three scores indicates what style of leadership you use most frequently. If your highest score is 40 or more, it is a very strong indicator of your preferred style.

- The **lowest** of the three scores is an indicator of the style you least use. If your lowest score is 20 or less, it is a very strong indicator you rarely use this style.

If there is only a small difference between the three scores, then this indicates that you have either a balanced approach to your leadership style (if the scores are mid-high), no clear perception of the mode you operate out of (if the scores are low), or you are a new leader and are trying to establish the correct style for you (if the scores are mid-low).

Now update your Learning Journal (page 85)

ACTIVITY 5: LEADERSHIP STYLE REFLECTIONS

Reflect on situations that you experienced as a leader. In the table below write examples of situations where you consider yourself as having been effective and others when you were less than effective (i.e. on reflection you would have chosen a different leadership style for the situation). For the ineffective examples, list the leadership style that would have been more effective.

Basic Style	Effective	Ineffective	Which Leadership Style would have been more effective?
Authoritarian			
Participative			
Delegative			

Now update your Learning Journal (page 85)

 To help you with this activity, download the job aid: **Leadership Styles Summary** from https://www.catherinematttiske.com/books

"Outstanding leaders go out of their way to boost the self-esteem of their personnel. If people believe in themselves, it's amazing what they can accomplish."

SAM WALTON

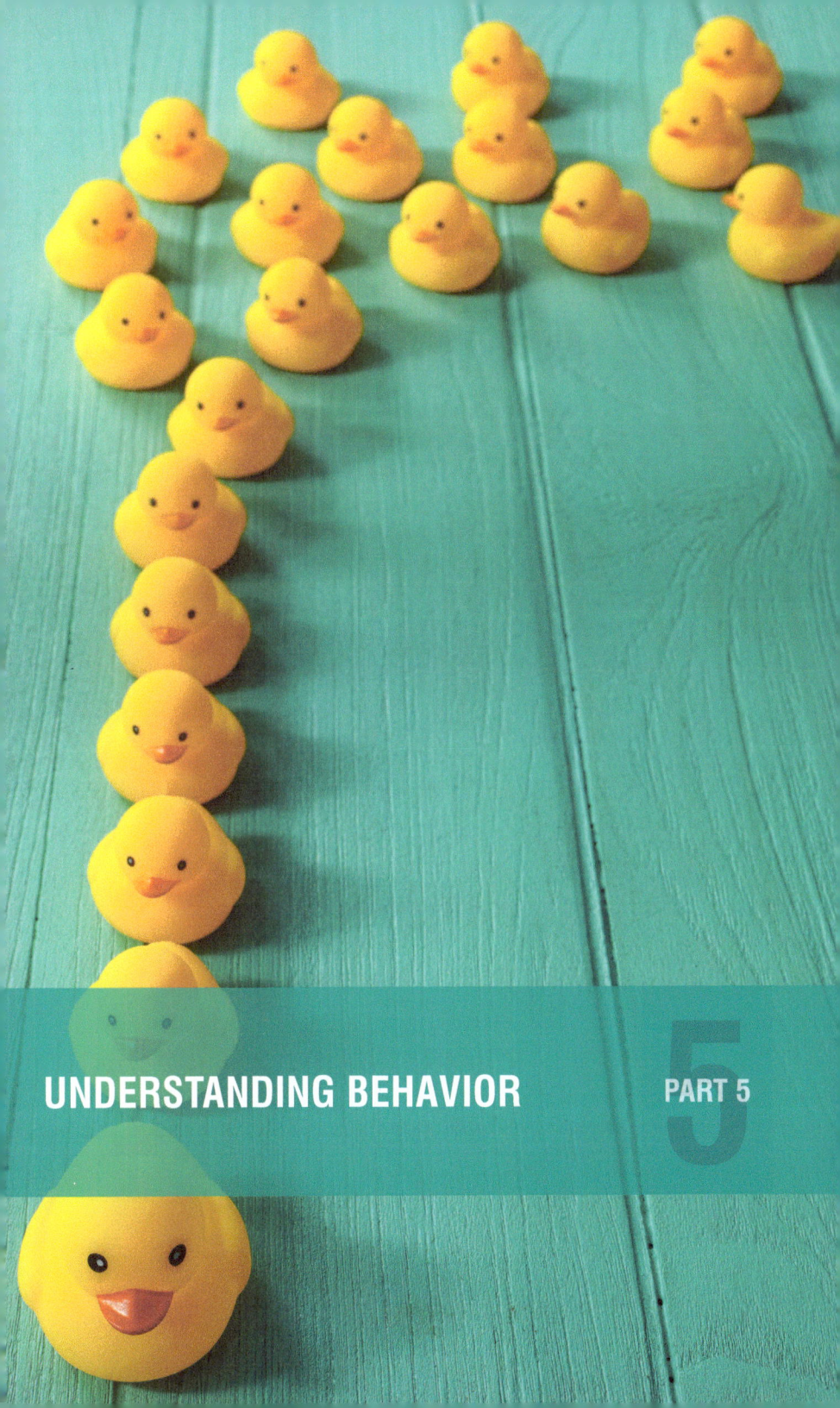

UNDERSTANDING BEHAVIOR

PART 5

UNDERSTANDING BEHAVIOR

"The real leader has no need to lead - he is content to point the way."

HENRY MILLER

Values and Beliefs

Our values and beliefs are those things that are important to us. They drive what we think, say and do and are an insight into our individual personality.

Each of us has our own value system, elements of which we are very aware and some less so because we haven't thought about them lately.

Beliefs are mental constructs we create, based on our experience to help us make sense of the world in which we live.

Values and beliefs support the individual's sense of identity, i.e. the who behind the why, how, what, where and when, and relate to the deeper motivations which drive people to act or persevere.

When a leader works with a member of their team at the value and belief level, it is at these higher levels that it is possible to fully unlock the potential for performance and behavior change.

Beliefs

Beliefs drive behavior. Mark Twain wrote "if you believe you can, you can and if you believe you can't you're right".

Our Beliefs were being formed from the moment we were born. It all starts with a vague representation of something we experience which is added to by even more experience, and solidifies. The sum of our experiences becomes a 'knowing', something that we consider to be true. If more validating and affirming experiences are added the belief develops even further into a conviction. From that point on we have built a fortress around the belief and it might seem that no-one is able to prove the belief wrong.

Beliefs can, and do, change but the belief that beliefs are changeable is in itself a challenging belief for some people because they think of beliefs as possessions. People talk about 'having' and 'holding' beliefs. We also have a personal investment in our beliefs; when the world confirms them then it makes sense to us, and gives us a sense of security and certainty. "I told you so" is a satisfying phrase, not because we wanted anything to go wrong, but because our beliefs were proved right.

John Stuart Mill wrote "One person with a belief is equal to a force of 99 who have only interests" and there are many people in history who are testimony to that being the case. People who have changed history - Columbus, Einstein, Ghandi, Churchill - have changed peoples beliefs.

Belief delivers a direct command to one's nervous system. When you believe something is true, you literally go into the state of it being true. Handled effectively, beliefs can be the most powerful forces for leaders to tap into and influence.

Limiting Beliefs

Limiting beliefs are the major culprits stopping us achieving our goals and living our values. They act as rules that stop us getting what is possible, what we are capable of and what we deserve. When a client has limiting beliefs their behavior is not what they want but they think they cannot change it. As their leader we need to ensure that followers change, replace or discard limiting beliefs. When a coach asks "What stops you from achieving your goal?" the answers very often are limiting beliefs.

As stated earlier, limiting beliefs may come from childhood, perhaps copied from parents. These early beliefs often stay hidden and we do not consciously evaluate them as adults.

Some typical limiting beliefs are:

'No pain, no gain'
'I can't work a computer'
'Other people are better than me'
'I'm too old to go to the gym'

Limiting beliefs will make a person 'give up' rather than change their strategy and take action until they succeed.

Do beliefs guarantee results every time? Of course not. However, history has shown time and again that if people maintain the belief system that empowers them, they will come back with enough action and resourcefulness to succeed eventually.

Working with Different Needs and Goals

Each of your team members has different needs and goals. Your role as their leader is to create an environment that works for individuals.

The following shows five ways to assist:

1) **Be clear on expectations up front**
   Let people know what is important to you and what you expect from them.

2) **Walk the talk and lead by example**
   Step in to support your team at every opportunity. Maintain your own sense of personal integrity at all times.

3) **Get to know your people and what makes them tick**
   Be a student of understanding differences, and adapt your style to meet their needs. Provide opportunities for people to operate from their strengths.

4) **Provide honest feedback and continuous coaching**
   Encourage an environment where team members can learn from one another, including from you, and you from them. Tell the truth.

5) **Encourage and reward accountability**
   Provide reinforcement when people take initiative. Be a driver of personal accountability. Admit mistakes and learn from them.

Complete Activity # 6
Team Behavior - Leadership Language

ACTIVITY 6: TEAM BEHAVIOR - LEADERSHIP LANGUAGE

The following table lists five ways to assist the leader to meet team needs and goals. For each, write two phrases or questions you might use to begin a conversation that leads you in the listed direction.

For example, if you want to begin a conversation about your expectations of your team, you might say "To start our meeting today, let's start with a project update on ABC project" or ask "How are we tracking against our project plan for ABC project?"

	Write two phrases or questions you might use to being a conversation in this direction.
Be clear on expectations up front. Let people know what is important to you and what you expect from them.	
Walk the talk and lead by example. Step in to support your team at every opportunity. Maintain your own sense of personal integrity at all times.	
Get to know your people and what makes them tick. Be a student of understanding differences, and adapt your style to meet their needs. Provide opportunities for people to operate from their strengths.	
Provide honest feedback, and continuous coaching. Encourage an environment where team members can learn from one another, including from you, and you from them. Tell the truth.	
Encourage and reward accountability. Provide reinforcement when people take initiative. Be a driver of personal accountability. Admit mistakes and learn from them.	

Now update your Learning Journal (page 85)

LEADERSHIP & ROLES

PART 6

LEADERSHIP & THE THEORY OF ROLES

Another way of understanding your team is in terms of the roles each team member adopts. This is based on the premise that people within groups tend to act in certain ways and take on certain responsibilities.

Over a period of time, everyone in the group will find their own role. It is unwise to pigeon-hole someone's behavior because they can have one or many roles and change according to the situation.

Likely Team Roles

The Innovator

The member of the team who likes to have new ideas. He or she can be helpful, or very disruptive, especially if the person refuses to do things by the book. Beware of dismissing their ideas - this will lead to resentment, or will make you look ineffective. Often a good way of neutralizing rogue ideas is to have them discussed in meetings.

The Critic

Every team needs someone they can trust to evaluate and test new ideas in a proactive and productive way. If you're lucky (or skilful) the Critic will spend their time neutralizing ideas proposed by the Innovator. Never be too worried by the productive critic - the unproductive negative critic is the problem.

The Loner

Loners don't like going with the group. Some people are happiest working by themselves, and sometimes the Loner can even help the rest of the team pull together. However, don't leave Loners to their own devices: Loners need a team and can become de-motivated if left out.

The Guardian of the Norms

Guardians have one of the most important roles in the team. Their function is to be authorities on the established way of doing things, group customs and procedures, rather like "village elders'. Sometimes the leader performs this role, sometimes it is the role of a long standing and methodical team member. Guardians can set standards, but they can also become opponents of change. In times of change, you should try to enlist (or neutralise) the Guardian.

The Joker

Every team needs someone who will raise a laugh and relieve tension. Don't worry about Jokers unless they become "Showboaters" who like to spend time big-noting themselves rather than completing productive work.

The Team Player

This role is the one taken by someone who is happiest when conforming to the team's expectations and will respond well to any call for "Team Effort". However, don't assume that the Team Player is necessarily any more motivated than, say, the Loner.

The Weakling

The person who struggles to keep up with the rest. Sometimes this is due to genuine weaknesses - in skill or knowledge. Often it is because the person has a "mental block": you may need to show them they can succeed and motivate them by allowing them to 'win' and build confidence.

The Problem Child

Often motivated by a desire for attention, the Problem Child may deliberately fail to do some simple task, or may be deliberately unruly so that termination may seem the only solution.

Sometimes the Problem Child is a popular team member and can fulfil the same role as the Joker, acting as a catalyst or source of inspiration. Dismissing such a person, even if justifiable, can lead to resentment. Through performance counselling, the effective leader will satisfy their need for attention in another way and help them switch into a more productive role.

The Helper

Sometimes invaluable - the people who take it upon themselves to welcome new team members, explain techniques and report any problems. Sometimes they are extremely disruptive, for exactly the same reasons, and can make mountains out of molehills, or can "help" teammates adopt bad habits. They can also use their time spent "helping" as an excuse for their own poor performance.

The Bully

Someone who delights in picking on other team members or making jokes at their expense. Reasons for this may be insecurity, fear of failure, pride, or just plain old-fashioned aggression. Interestingly enough, some successful people seem to enjoy playing the Bully. You have to decide what is acceptable and what is unacceptable. Never let a Bully bully you. Meet their threats calmly, logically and forcefully.

The Sergeant Major

Identifying a Sergeant Major can make a valuable contribution. Some people naturally enjoy seeing a team "pulling together" and will automatically take responsibility for maintaining standards, keeping a watchful eye and so on. If you have a Sergeant Major in your team put them to good use. Otherwise, they may turn into Rebel Leaders.

The Rebel Leader

Every manager's nightmare is the popular team member who becomes the team's unofficial spokesperson. Note that trying to remove a Rebel Leader will usually create more problems than it solves. Often Rebel Leaders arise because of genuine grievances or problems that need addressing and this should be your first priority.

It is probably better not to consult with the Rebel Leader on a one to one basis as this may only enhance their position (although counselling in private is a good idea).

A better way is to lead a discussion group and get straight to the heart of the problem. Devise an alternative, which will enable you to regain the initiative. Sometimes, Rebel Leaders are merely excusing their own poor performance or their dissatisfaction with their position, in which case they should be set strict performance related targets.

Applying the Theory

The theory of roles is helpful because almost every team does seem to create these characters. For instance, if a team's Problem Child leaves, very often another team member will take on that role. Very often one person can fulfil a variety of roles (a person might be Joker, Problem Child, Rebel Leader all rolled into one).

We can draw the following conclusions:

- If you have a problem with a team member, the problem may lie with that person, elsewhere in the team, or with your leadership.

- Although you can try to channel behavior, you must recognise you may never be able to eradicate certain roles within a team unless you change your own behavior. For example, you might remove the need for there to be a Helper if you are more helpful and approachable.

- It is wrong to think about team members just as individuals. If you want to motivate them, you must first motivate the whole team.

 **Complete Activity # 7**
Team Roles

ACTIVITY 7: TEAM ROLES

In the table below list the names of each of your team members. For each, list role/s that they currently hold within the team. Use the Likely Team Roles list (pages 50-53) as a guide and add other roles of your own making as required.

Then identify whether you will aim to enhance, modify, or diminish the role so that your personal and organizational goals are maximized for success.

In the last column, identify your first step in making the changes.

Team Member	Role	Role Change Required?	First Action Step

ACTIVITY 7: CONTINUED

Team Member	Role	Role Change Required?	First Action Step

Now update your Learning Journal (page 85)

LEADING A TEAM

PART 7

LEADING A TEAM

"Great leaders are almost always great simplifiers, who can cut through argument, debate, and doubt to offer a solution everybody can understand."

GENERAL COLIN POWELL

5 Stages of Group Development

Stage 1: Forming

In the **Forming** stage, personal relations are characterized by dependence. Group members rely on safe, patterned behavior and look to the group leader for guidance and direction. Group members have a desire for acceptance by the group and a need to know that the group is safe.

Members attempt to become oriented to the tasks as well as to one another. Discussion centers around defining the scope of the task, how to approach it, and similar concerns. To grow from this stage to the next, each member must relinquish the comfort of non-threatening topics and risk the possibility of conflict.

Stage 2: Storming

Storming is characterized by competition and conflict. As the group members attempt to organise for the task, conflict inevitably results in their personal relations. Individuals have to bend and mould their feelings, ideas, attitudes, and beliefs to suit the group. Because of "fear of exposure" or "fear of failure," there will be an increased desire for structural clarification and commitment. Although conflicts may or may not surface as group issues, they do exist. Questions will arise about who is going to be responsible for what, what the rules are, what the reward system is, and what criteria for evaluation are.

In order to progress to the next stage, group members must move from a "testing and proving" mentality to a problem-solving mentality. The most important trait in helping groups to move on to the next stage seems to be the ability to listen.

"Effective leadership is not about making speeches or being liked; leadership is defined by results not attributes."

PETER DRUCKER

Stage 3: Norming

In the **Norming** stage, interpersonal relations are characterized by cohesion. Members are willing to change their preconceived ideas or opinions based on facts presented by other members, and they actively ask questions of each another. Leadership is shared, and cliques dissolve. It is during this stage of development (assuming the group gets this far) that people begin to experience a sense of group belonging and a feeling of relief as a result of resolving interpersonal conflicts. They feel good about being part of an effective group.

> "The pessimist complains about the wind.
> The optimist expects it to change.
> The leader adjusts the sails."
>
> JOHN MAXWELL

Stage 4: Performing

The **Performing** stage is not reached by all groups. If group members are able to evolve to stage four, their capacity, range, and depth of personal relations expand to true interdependence. In this stage, people can work independently, in subgroups, or as a total unit. By now, the group should be most productive. There is unity: group identity is complete, group morale is high, and group loyalty is intense. The overall goal is productivity through problem solving and work.

Stage 5: Adjourning

The final stage, **Adjourning**, involves the termination of tasks and disengagement from relationships. A planned conclusion usually includes recognition for participation and achievement and an opportunity for members to say personal goodbyes.

MANAGING TEAM MEETINGS - GETTING THE MOST FROM EVERYONE

Step 1 - Plan the Meeting

Before we meet…

90% of an effective meeting happens before it takes place. Even the briefest most informal meeting will benefit from preparation. A more formal meeting involving more than a few people must be organized thoroughly.

A survey of business managers who say they always:

- Define the meeting's purpose   66%
- Address each item on the agenda   62%
- Assign follow-up action   59%
- Take minutes of the meeting   47%
- Invite only essential participants   46%
- Write an agenda with time frames   36%

There is significant room for improvement, to increase meeting effectiveness.

Meeting Timetable

Suggested timings from preparation, to day of meeting, to follow up for an In-person meeting. Timings for Virtual meetings may be shorter than those stated.

Task	Day	Action
Notice of Meeting	-10	Chair / Administrator
Participant additions to the agenda and submission of papers	-7	Participants
Agenda agreed and distributed	-6	Chair / Administrator
Day of meeting	0	All
Minutes distributed	+2	Administrator

Step 2 - Prepare the Agenda

Every meeting should have an agenda and it should be given in advance to each participant. Ideally, participants should have an opportunity to contribute to an agenda prior to the meeting.

Whoever controls the agenda controls the meeting. If there is no stated public agenda, the meeting may be overrun by private agendas. The result will be confusion, frustration and failure.

A written agenda allows everyone to focus on what they are to do before, during and after the meeting. It acts as:

- A plan of the meeting to aid preparation
- An objective control of the meeting's purpose
- A measure of the meeting's success

Agenda Essentials

The agenda should indicate what will happen at the meeting. The most formal of agendas will include, in this order:

- The title of the meeting
- Date, time, venue
- Apologies for absence
- Minutes of the previous meeting
- Matters arising from the previous meeting
- Reports from sub-committees
- Other items to be discussed
- Contributions from guest speakers / consultants
- The date, time, and venue of the next meeting.

> **KEEP ENERGY LEVELS UP**
>
> Schedule a break for meetings longer than 1 ½ hours. 15-minute breaks should be taken every 60-90 minutes.

Step 3 - Conducting the Meeting

Things to include...

- Take Minutes
- Create a strong opening
- Use Visual Aids
- Encourage discussion by using questions
- Handle difficult situations
- Handle conflict

More on Encouraging discussion by using Questions

 # 1 Asking for feelings and opinions

Use a method of asking questions that will help people express their ideas, draw people out, and encourage discussion.

For example

- What is your reaction to...?
- How do you feel about...?
- What is your thinking on...?
- What brings you to conclude that...?
- What are some other ways to get...?

Do not say:

2 Paraphrase

One way to help people reach mutual understanding is to paraphrase, that is, to ask one person to repeat what someone else said and to state what that person meant:

- Are you asking me to…?
- Let me see if I understand your position. Are you saying that…?
- Before we go on, let me paraphrase what I think you are proposing…
- Let me restate you last point to see if I understand.
- Before you go on, do you mean that…?

Do not say:

What he/she means is…

3 Encourage Participation

Sometimes people tend to hold back. They can be encouraged to participate by such questions as:

- Lee, how do you feel about this?
- Austin, how would you answer Sam's question?
- Before we go on, I would like to hear from Brook on this.
- We have heard from everyone but Jane. Jane, what is your feeling on this?
- We haven't heard from Jack yet. Jack, what is your opinion here?

Do not:

Spotlight shy Participant

Do not:

Allow people to endlessly chat

4 Ask for a Summary

- Many good ideas have been presented in the last few minutes. Will someone please summarize the major points before we go on?
- I have heard a number of proposals. Bill, will you summarize what has been agreed upon?
- It is clear Jim does not agree. Jim, will you summarize your major objections.
- I have lost track. Let's summarize what has been done so far.

Do not:

Ignore those who seem lost in the conversation

5 Ask for Clarification

- I didn't understand your last comment. What would you do if…?
- The examples you gave concern week day operations - do they also affect weekends?
- I saw Kate shaking her head. Kate would it help if we took a minute to explain the history?

Do not:

Don't cut short idea generation and brain-storming

6 Explore an idea in more detail

- What are some other ways to approach this problem?
- Are there other things we should consider?
- Tan, what would you add to what has been said?

7 Be Supporting

- Let's give Tony a chance to tell it the way he sees it.
- Dave, you have had your say. Now it's Graham's turn. Give him a chance to explain.
- That's a good point, thanks Heather.

Do not:

Don't ignore participants that are not contributing

8 Question Assumptions

- Your proposal assumes that unless we use threats, they won't cooperate. Is that right?
- Your suggestion assumes that we can't meet the schedule. Is that correct?
- Your objection assumes that we will not get promised deliveries. Is that a good assumption?
- We mustn't make decisions on their behalf. Let's survey their opinions and discuss the results next meeting.

Do not:

Let broad-brush comments and suggestions pass through

Complete Activity # 8
Meeting Planner

Complete Activity # 9
Meeting Agenda

ACTIVITY 8: MEETING PLANNER

Download the **TPC Meeting Planner** from https://www.catherinemattiske.com/books

Activity using the TPC Meeting Planner

Download the TPC Meeting Planner and use it for your next meeting.

Now update your Learning Journal (page 85)

ACTIVITY 9: MEETING AGENDA

 Download the **TPC Meeting Agenda** from https://www.catherinemattiske.com/books

Activity using the TPC Meeting Agenda

Download the TPC Meeting Agenda and use it for your next meeting.

Now update your Learning Journal (page 85)

PERSONAL AND GROUP MOTIVATION

Introduction to Motivation

The ability to motivate staff is the essential ingredient of all good leaders. In order to get individuals to achieve personal and group targets, motivation is particularly important. Consequently, a leader who cannot motivate his or her team to perform is likely to not achieve personal or organizational goals.

1) Motivation comes through good leadership.

All great leaders in business, politics and history have been superb motivators *because* they were great leaders, not the other way around. If you can capture your team's imagination and excitement, they will be motivated. If you lose their respect, you will lose their motivation.

2) There is no single theory of human motivation.

There are many good theories of motivation. This doesn't mean that these theories cannot give us profound insights into human nature, but we shouldn't be afraid of drawing our own conclusions and acting on them. The best place to learn about the motivation of your team is by listening to them and understanding them *as people*.

3) Motivation is ultimately to do with the self.

Motivation is never concerned with telling people to do what you want. It involves instead getting people to want the same thing as you, so they see your task as *their* task. This is vital in business where most things depend not on what you do, but on how you do it.

4) Motivation comes from your own belief and enthusiasm.

Your team will expect you to set the tone of their work: if you believe in your goals, your company and your products, so will they. If you do not, you will never be able to motivate them.

Herzberg's Hygiene Theory

Herzberg's theory is well respected as it recognizes there are two factors that affect motivation - *motivators* and *hygiene factors*. He found that when people felt dissatisfied with their jobs, they were concerned about the environment in which they were working. On the other hand, when people felt good about their jobs, this feeling had to do with the work itself.

Herzberg called the first category of needs hygiene (or maintenance) factors. *Hygiene* because they describe people's environment and service the primary function of preventing job dissatisfaction; *maintenance* because they are never completely satisfied - they have to continue to be maintained. He called the second category of needs *motivators* because they seemed to be effective in motivating people to superior performance.

Herzberg's theory helps us make sense of how to motivate people and keep them motivated. It also shows us how such intangible things as poor office decorations or the wretched state of the company canteen can gradually *de-motivate* people.

Motivators:

Provide staff with positive motivation to do something. They include achievement, praise, and opportunity for growth, job satisfaction and interest. If you do not offer your staff these motivators, they will not be motivated.

Hygiene Factors:

Do not, in themselves motivate. They provide the right **environment** for staff to be motivated. They include adequate pay, working environment, administrative back up, company policy, atmosphere. If hygiene factors are non-existent, it will be difficult to motivate your team no matter what motivators you use.

MOTIVATOR	HYGIENE FACTOR
The Job Itself	*Environment*
Achievement	Policies and Administration
Recognition for Accomplishment	Supervision
Challenging Work	Working Conditions
Increased Responsibility	Interpersonal Relations
Growth and Development	Money, Status, Security

Motivators found in the workplace

Pride

Most people by pride to some extent. If nothing else you must:

- Encourage them to take pride in their work.
- Make your staff feel their effort is important.
- Let them know you value their skills.

Use phrases such as 'set the right example', 'I can count on you', 'the others will take their lead from you'. However, don't overflatter: feel free to use such criticisms as 'I was surprised by your actions…', 'I want to talk to you before your behavior becomes a problem', and so on. Don't belittle the pride motivated person - it can lead to resentment, or even resignation.

Peer Group Pressure

The person motivated by peer group pressure does not want:

- To let the side down.
- Be the odd one out.
- The lowest performer.

Use phrases like 'the team are counting on you', 'we can all do this together'. They are unlikely to be the one to initiate action.

Interest

Involve this person in problem solving. Ask for their ideas. Leave tasks open-ended. Offer opportunities to gain product knowledge or training.

Security

Show that by doing what you are asking:

- They will become more secure.
- Their lives easier.
- Their work more predictable.

Someone with a great need for security will particularly dislike any system that exposes him or her to failure or managerial scrutiny. Provide routines and structure. Regularly reassure staff that they are doing well.

Loyalty

- Encourage and reward with praise and recognition.
- Never take people for granted.
- Be loyal to your staff.

People often leave jobs because they don't feel their manager repaid their loyalty.

Habit

Most of us do most things for no better reason than habit. Habit also makes us reluctant to change. Overcome habit by managing change sensitively. Encourage good habits by establishing routines for your staff.

Greed

Show how your advice, encouragement and so on will help your staff earn more money. Praise high earners and never make them feel "guilty". Only beware: don't let people cut corners for quick results or give up if results are slow in coming. Never insult someone by assuming that his or her only interest is money.

Power

Offer people some power over their environment, or show how they can achieve power if they are successful. Power means:

- Control over their work (e.g. sales territory).
- A position of team leading.
- The personal freedom that comes with higher earnings.
- The power which comes from getting a customer to say "YES!"

Competitive Spirit

- Encourage competition with praise and prizes.
- Focus and channel competitive natures by showing them *where* they can compete successfully.

For instance: 'you could be our best telemarketer'; 'you could have the best kept records in the team'; 'it's between you and Pete for the best figures this afternoon'.

Don't make work too competitive: people can resent having to compete against each other pointlessly; others can shy away from competitions. People only want to compete for things that they might win that are worth winning.

Desire to be liked

Wanting to be liked is a very common emotion. Sometimes it can be counter productive in sales, as it can make staff reluctant to "upset" their customers by pushing for business. It does have its positive side: people will want to please you and want to be good team members.

Desire to be helpful

If someone is keen to help, harness this energy: can the person induct trainees or collect data for you? Present comments in such language as 'could you help me with this?'; 'I don't find your current attitude very helpful'; 'what ideas do you have…?'

Desire for praise or recognition

- Be keen to bestow praise - whenever it is deserved.
- Never praise indiscriminately - always explain why you are praising.
- Reinforce the good performance, show sincerity.

Whenever you praise, pause for a second to let them enjoy your praise. Establish eye contact; smile warmly. Never praise grudgingly. Praise staff in front of managers and team members.

Excitement

Be fun and dynamic *yourself*. Don't always do the predictable. Encourage spontaneity.

Ease

Most people prefer the easy option. Harness this as best you can: make it easy for staff to do things "by the book"; introduce changes smoothly. Beware of short cuts.

Fear

Managers often use fear needlessly or because they themselves are afraid to confront the real problem: sometimes it is easier to threaten to dismiss a poor performer than to be honest and tell them the reasons for their poor performance.

Rather than fear for fear's sake, give fear a purpose - set the person clear precise goals which are *achievable*, and when they have achieved, give praise.

Complete Activity # 10
Your Motivators

ACTIVITY 10: YOUR MOTIVATORS

Break down what each of these needs mean to you. Analyze your own needs by completing the following table.

On a scale of 1 - 5, ✔ in each box which of the following motivates you the most.
(1 being the highest motivator and 5 being the lowest motivator)

STAFF MOTIVATION QUESTIONNAIRE

NAME:	Highest				Lowest
	1	2	3	4	5
Pride					
Peer Group Pressure					
Interest					
Loved Ones					
Security					
Loyalty					
Habit					
Greed					
Power					
Competitive Spirit					
To be Liked					
To be Helpful					
Praise					
Excitement					
Ease					
Fear					

Add others here - remember do not add hygiene factors, such as money. What you do **with the money** is the motivator.

Now update your Learning Journal (page 85)

Motivation and Money

Why might people want to earn more money?

Pride:	The employee equates what they earn with their worth as a person.
Peer Group:	The employee wants more money because their friends just had a pay rise.
Greed:	The employee just loves money!
Power:	The employee feels more powerful and has more control over their living conditions.
Comfort:	They love to eat out and buy luxuries.
Care for Loved Ones:	They want to treat the children to a holiday.
Peace of Mind:	They don't want to worry about cash flow.

The point to be learned here is that instead of relying on money to keep our staff enthusiastic and committed, we should be motivating our staff in other ways. For instance:

Pride:	Might be better motivated if they are offered a new job title, or given public recognition.
Peer Group:	Tell them how essential they are to the team, or they may be motivated by a company party.
Greed:	Bonus, new Commission incentive will produce more than a simple pay rise.
Power:	A Promotion or some sort of responsibility or administrative function may satisfy this need.
Comfort:	A Dining or Clothes allowance - it will be less than a pay rise.
Care:	More interest in families, medical insurance or long-term prospects.
Peace:	Give employees other sources of security: offer praise, say what they need to make their position secure.

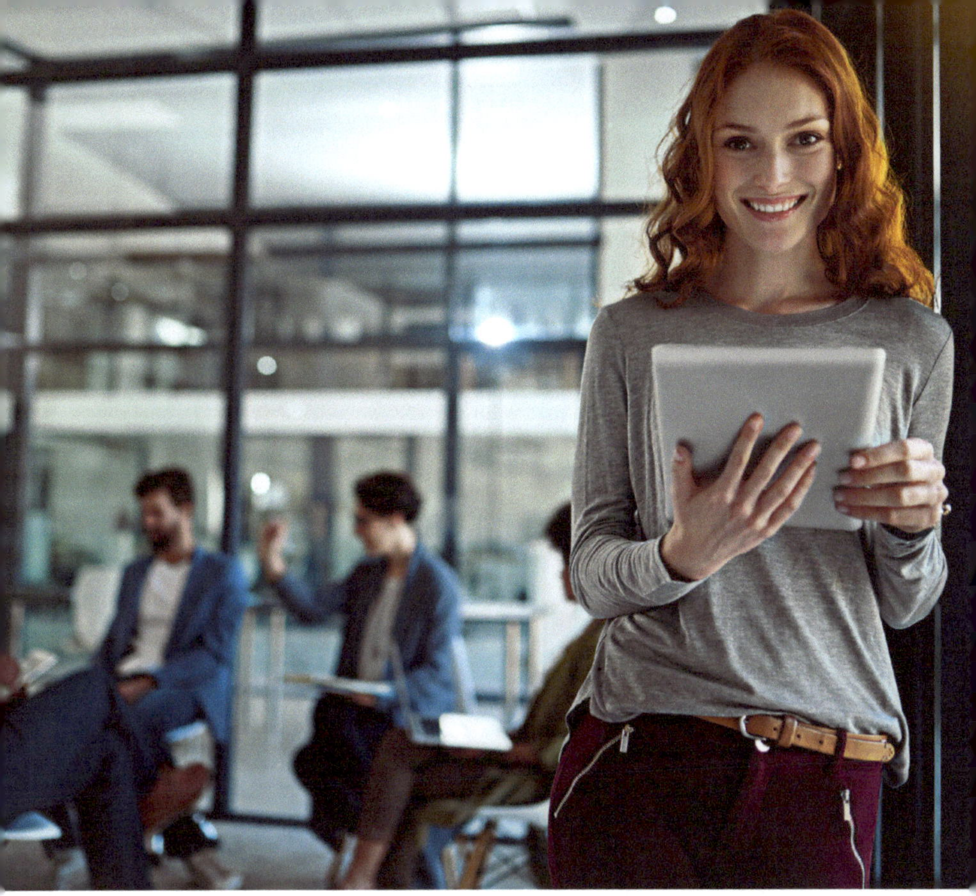

STOP

Complete Activity # 11

Analyzing Team Motivation

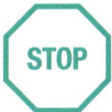

STOP

Complete Activity # 12

Motivating Ways

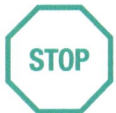

STOP

Complete Activity # 13

Inspiring Through Vision

ACTIVITY 11: ANALYZING TEAM MOTIVATION

A useful activity is to try to analyze each of your staff's motivations. This activity focuses on true Motivators not Hygiene Factors. Use the reference guide to help with a list of motivators.

When complete, reflect on the results. Use this as a basis for getting to know your staff better and targeting their motivators. As your understanding of your staff deepens, you can start to make notes on their motivators and build these into your reward and recognition strategy and performance review processes.

Team Member Name	Motivator - in your opinion

Warning!
While this can give us useful insights, we must try not to play the amateur psychologist. Beware of pigeon holing staff in ways which bear no relationship to reality, such as "Bill's prime motivation is pride, Mary just wants to fit in, Gary wants enough money to buy a sports car", and so on.

Now update your Learning Journal (page 85)

ACTIVITY 12: MOTIVATING WAYS

(a) Motivating Ways

Other than motivating by money, how could you be motivating your team in other ways?

1. Pride: _____

2. Peer Group: _____

3. Greed: _____

4. Power: _____

5. Comfort: _____

6. Care for Loved Ones: _____

7. Peace of Mind: _____

(b) Planning for Motivation

What steps can you take to reduce the risk of lack of motivation within your team?

_____
_____

What practical steps can you take to increase the motivation of the individuals on your team?

_____
_____

Now update your Learning Journal (page 85)

ACTIVITY 13: INSPIRING THROUGH VISION

Complete the following incorporating all sections of what you have learned so far. Thinking "I will…" or "I could…." will help prompt your thoughts.

Communicate where my business is going by:	
Help people understand how they can contribute to where our business is going by:	
Seek new ways of doing things to achieve our goals by:	
Support team through using different leadership styles by:	
Recognise different roles team members adopt by:	
Motivate individuals and my team by:	

Now update your Learning Journal (page 85)

Section 2

LEARNING JOURNAL

The Learning Journal is used throughout the process to record your key learnings, hot tips and things to remember.

Update your Learning Journal at anytime. Ensure you complete your Learning Journal after you finish each activity. Then turn back to the Learning Short-take® to continue your learning.

LEARNING JOURNAL

As you work through this Learning Short-take®, make detailed notes on this page of the lessons you have learned and any useful skill areas. For each lesson or refresher point think about how you could further develop this skill. Your coach will want to discuss these with you in your Skill Development Action Planning meeting.

> "…that is what learning is.
> You suddenly understand something you've understood all your life, but in a new way."
> DORIS LESSING

> "Act as though it were impossible to fail."
> WINSTON CHURCHILL

"The wise do at once what the fool does later."
BALTASAR GRACIAN (1601-58), SPANISH JESUIT PRIEST AND AUTHOR.

Learning or Idea	Action to be taken	Result Expected

Learning Journal - continued

Learning or Idea	Action to be taken	Result Expected

"Anyone who stops learning is old, whether at twenty or eighty."
HENRY FORD

Learning or Idea	Action to be taken	Result Expected

❝

*"If there is a trait which does characterize leaders it is opportunism. Successful people are very often those who steadfastly refuse to be daunted
by disadvantage and have the ability to turn disadvantage to good effect.
They are people who seize opportunity and take risks. Leadership then seems to be a matter of personality and character."*

JOHN VINEY

❞

Section 3

SKILL DEVELOPMENT ACTION PLAN

Your Skill Development Action Plan is the last Step in the process. After you have completed the Learning Short-take® and all Activities, update your Learning Journal, then complete this section.

SKILL DEVELOPMENT ACTION PLAN

This is the most important part of the program - your individual Skill Development Action Plan.

You need to complete this plan before meeting with your manager or prior to on-going coaching. You will discuss it in detail with your manager or coach as he or she will ensure that you have everything you need to complete the tasks and activities.

Once you have completed your **Skill Development Action Plan** schedule a meeting time with your manager or coach to review your plan. Take your Learning Short-take® and all other documentation received during the training course to this meeting.

Remember - you have committed to your **Skill Development Action Plan**, and need to make time to complete your tasks!

> *"The mind, once stretched by a new idea, never regains its original dimensions."*
> OLIVER WENDELL HOLMES

> *"Whatever you can do or dream you can - begin it. Boldness has genius, power and magic."*
> JOHANN WOLFGANG VON GOETHE

"Imagination is the eye of the soul."
JOSEPH JOUBERT (1754-1824)

Task or activity (Be specific)	Measure (this will help you to know you have achieved it)	Date (Be specific)
Reflect on your Learning Journal. Transfer action items that you can apply to your job. Ensure that you include some 'stretch goals' and also a blend of short, medium and long term goals.	Apart from you, who else is needed to assist you in achieving your goal.	Be specific. A general date such as 'Quarter 1', 'August', or 'by end of year' is vague and more likely to result in not achieving your target. Be specific – e.g. 22nd November.

IDEAS FOR DISCUSSION WITH MY MANAGER

Ideas

CONGRATULATIONS!

You've now completed this Learning Short-take®.

Meet with your Manager/Coach to discuss your
Skill Development Action Plan.

"

"Surround yourself with the best people
you can find, delegate authority,
and don't interfere as long as the policy you've
decided upon is being carried out."

RONALD REAGAN

QUICK REFERENCE

This Quick Reference provides you with a summary of key concepts, models and reference material from Learning Short-takes®. We have also included some quotations to ponder.

Use this section as a quick reference to keep your learning active.

Quick Reference

> **"Managers are people who do things right, while leaders are people who do the right thing."**
>
> Warren Bennis, Ph.D.

Leadership

Leadership is the process of directing the behavior of others toward the accomplishment of some common objectives. Leadership is influencing people to get things done willingly to a standard and quality above their norm.

Quick Reference

Management vs Leadership

Management	Leadership
Day-to-Day Operational Tasks	Influencing for Long-term Achievement

> **Leader is a label we give to an individual who holds a vision and courageously pursues that vision in such a way that it resonates with the psyche of people.**

Quick Reference

What is Your Vision?

Everyday, strive to achieve one more step towards your Vision.

> **The leader's task is to create an environment that is conducive to self-motivation.**
>
> Nido Quebin

Leadership Style

Choose the best style for each situation:

- Authoritarian
- Participative
- Delegative

> **A business is a reflection of the leader.**
>
> Gary Feldmar

Quick Reference

Working with Different Needs & Goals

- Be clear on expectations up front
- Walk the talk and lead by example
- Get to know your people and what makes them tick
- Provide honest feedback and continuous coaching
- Encourage and reward accountability

> **Vision without action is merely a dream. Action without vision just passes the time. Vision with action can change the world.**

Joel Barker - Power of Vision

Quick Reference

5 Stages of Group Development

Stage 1 - Forming

Stage 2 - Storming

Stage 3 - Norming

Stage 4 - Performing

Stage 5 - Adjourning

Managing Team Meetings

Suggested timing for an In-person meeting. Timings for Virtual meetings may be shorter than those stated.

Task	Day	Action
Notice of Meeting	- 10	Chair / Administrator
Participant additions to the agenda and submission of papers	- 7	Participants
Agenda agreed and distributed	- 6	Chair / Administrator
Day of meeting	0	All
Minutes distributed	+ 2	Administrator

Quick Reference

Motivating Your Team

MOTIVATOR The Job Itself	HYGIENE FACTOR Environment
Achievement	Policies and Administration
Recognition for Accomplishment	Supervision
	Working Conditions
Challenging Work	Interpersonal Relations
Increased Responsibility	Money, Status, Security
Growth and Development	

Money is not the Motivator.

Money is a Hygiene Factor.

To help determine the motivator ask: **What does my employee spend their money on?**

Quick Reference

> **The greater the loyalty of a group toward the group, the greater is the motivation among the members to achieve the goals of the group, and the greater the probability that the group will achieve its goals.**
>
> Rensis Likert

Leading the Team

Identify team roles & influence your team members to change any unproductive roles into ones that help meet your goals.

Quick Reference

Reflect on your Leadership

Leadership takes consistent effort.

Create the time for reflection and planning.

NEXT STEPS

Congratulations! You have now completed this Learning Short-take® title. The entire list of Learning Short-takes® can be found on the catherinemattiske.com website.

In this section we have suggested Learning Short-take® titles for you that will build your learning. You may order these Learning Short-takes® online at https://www.catherinemattiske.com/books or from your bookstores.

Influencing for Opportunity
Identify and Maximize Ways to Influence

Course Content

- Part 1: Fundamentals of Influence
- Part 2: Influence: A Choice
- Part 3: Naturally Occurring Influence Patterns
- Part 4: Methods of Persuasion
- Part 5: The Challenges of Influence
- Part 6: Building a life of Influence

Learning Short-take® Outline

Influencing for Opportunity combines self-study with realistic workplace activities to provide you with the key skills and techniques to influence those around you. You will learn the theory of influence, influence principles and strategies, as well as how to plan and prepare for important opportunities to influence. As a result, you should achieve greater results in your organization, work more productively and effectively in a team environment, and develop stronger working relationships with co-workers, suppliers and customers.

The ability to influence others is critical in today's competitive business environment. Being highly skilled in influence enables you to build the relationships you need to get results inside or outside the organization. Employees and managers alike cannot assume they have power over others - they must earn it through influence. Being an influential person is a skill that can be learned and practiced. **Influencing for Opportunity** will help you succeed in the modern corporate environment by increasing your ability to influence others.

Influencing for Opportunity includes a **toolkit of job aids and learning support tools** provided to you as free downloads.

Learning Objectives

- Identify patterns of influence.
- Evaluate how you currently use influence behaviors and identify areas for development.
- Develop influence behaviors for greater personal and business success.
- Establish clear and powerful influence goals.
- Increase influence to overcome resistance.
- Describe how to ask for and receive support.
- Design an approach for formal and informal influence situations; apply the approach to a real-life situation.
- Create a Skill Development Action Plan.

Creative Business Thinking
Developing the Skills for Thinking Outside the Box

Learning Short-take® Outline

Creative Business Thinking includes a library of brilliant creativity tools, fun activities, and challenging business scenarios. These will help to stretch your thinking by deliberately challenging existing perspectives and considering alternative ways of working.

Creative Business Thinking is packed with techniques for creative thinking and fun 'mind quiz' activities. **Creative Business Thinking** constructively challenges the status quo to enable new ideas to surface and solve problems in ways that may not initially come to mind.

Within each of us there exists an infinite capacity for creating ideas and nurturing them through to innovation. **Creative Business Thinking** emphasizes pragmatic tools and techniques to successfully unlock creative potential.

Creative Business Thinking includes the job aid **15 Creativity Techniques for Problem Solving**, and the **Creative Business Thinking Techniques Wall Chart**, provided to you as free downloadable tools.

Learning Objectives

- Undertake a self assessment in creativity.
- List personal and organizational creative contributions.
- Choose personal creative techniques to be used in the workplace.
- Match group creativity techniques with case study applications.
- Use six thinking hats to solve a business challenge.
- Create a plan for an upcoming team meeting employing creative thinking techniques.

Course Content

- Part 1: Creativity and lateral thinking
- Part 2: Unleash those creative forces
- Part 3: Personal creative thinking techniques
- Part 4: Tools for Creative Business Thinking
  - 6 thinking hats
  - Brainstorming
  - Metaphors
  - Cause & effect (Fishbone Diagram)
  - Work breakdown structure
  - 5 Why's
  - Different point of view
  - Concept mapping / Mind mapping
- Part 5: Answers

High Performance Learning
Creating Effective High Performance Learners

Learning Short-take® Outline

High Performance Learning is written for managers and training professionals.

For managers, **High Performance Learning** will assist you in ensuring that your team gets the most out of internal and external training courses and e-learning programs to help meet your personal, team and organizational goals. It provides managers with an understanding of their role in the training process and how they can ensure that team members apply what they have learned after training.

For learning and development professionals, **High Performance Learning** explores strategies to engage managers and key stakeholders with participants throughout the entire learning process – all with minimal effort for you and the manager!

High Performance Learning includes the **Pre-Learning Short-take® Manager Conversation Tool** and the **Post-Learning Short-take® Manager Conversation Tool**, provided as free downloads

Learning Objectives

- Analyze a self-assessment regarding Manager involvement before, during and after employees' learning and development
- Define each element of Mattiske's High Performance Learning Model™
- Complete a High Performance Learning Model™ matrix for a case study and actual scenario
- Coach employees throughout the learning process with the aim of creating high performance
- Use TPC tools to assist in before and after learning conversations
- Create a Skill Development Action Plan.

Course Content

- Part 1: The Managers Role in Learning & Development
- Part 2: Mattiske's High Performance Learning Model™
- Part 3: Providing Support & Influencing Motivation
- Part 4: Coaching Learners to High Performance
- Part 5: Motivating & Supporting Learners completing Learning Short-takes®
- Part 6: Managing Learning Short-takes® - A Step-by-step Guide

www.catherinemattiske.com

www.ingramcontent.com/pod-product-compliance
Lightning Source LLC
Chambersburg PA
CBHW042229090526
44587CB00001B/7